CHECKERBOARD BIOGRAPHY LIBRARY

U.S. PRESIDENTS

The
United States Presidents

WILLIAM MCKINLEY

ABDO Publishing Company

Megan M. Gunderson

visit us at
www.abdopublishing.com

Published by ABDO Publishing Company, 8000 West 78th Street, Edina, Minnesota 55439.
Copyright © 2009 by Abdo Consulting Group, Inc. International copyrights reserved in all
countries. No part of this book may be reproduced in any form without written permission from the
publisher. The Checkerboard Library™ is a trademark and logo of ABDO Publishing Company.

Printed in the United States.

Cover Photo: Getty Images
Interior Photos: American Political History p. 19; AP Images pp. 28, 29; Corbis pp. 16, 20, 23, 27;
    iStockphoto p. 32; Library of Congress pp. 5, 11, 13, 14, 18, 26; National Archives pp. 15, 25;
    Picture History pp. 9, 10, 21

Editor: Heidi M.D. Elston
Art Direction & Cover Design: Neil Klinepier
Interior Design: Neil Klinepier

Library of Congress Cataloging-in-Publication Data

Gunderson, Megan M., 1981-
  William McKinley / Megan M. Gunderson.
    p. cm.
  Includes index.
  ISBN 978-1-60453-466-5
  1. McKinley, William, 1843-1901--Juvenile literature. 2. Presidents--United States--Biography--
Juvenile literature. I. Title.

  E711.6.G86 2009
  973.8'8092--dc22
  [B]
                          2008025597

CONTENTS

WILLIAM MCKINLEY

William McKinley was the twenty-fifth president of the United States. Before entering politics, he served bravely in the American **Civil War**. He also worked as a teacher and a lawyer.

McKinley then got involved in government. He became a leading member of the **Republican** Party. First, he was elected to the U.S. House of Representatives. There, he focused on taxes and protecting American businesses. Later, he became governor of Ohio.

In 1896, McKinley was elected president. While in office, he led the country through the Spanish-American War. The nation acquired new territories. Americans also continued to experience a time of great prosperity. In 1900, McKinley easily won reelection. But only six months after his second term began, the popular president was **assassinated**.

TIMELINE

1843 - On January 29, William McKinley was born in Niles, Ohio.

1861 - The American Civil War began in April; in June, McKinley joined the Twenty-third Ohio Volunteer Infantry.

1862 - On September 17, McKinley took part in the Battle of Antietam.

1869 - McKinley was elected prosecuting attorney of Stark County, Ohio.

1871 - On January 25, McKinley married Ida Saxton; on December 25, McKinley's daughter Katherine was born.

1873 - McKinley's daughter Ida was born on April 1.

1876 - McKinley was elected to the U.S. House of Representatives.

1890 - In Congress, McKinley sponsored the McKinley Tariff Act.

1891 - McKinley was elected governor of Ohio.

1896 - McKinley was elected the twenty-fifth U.S. president.

1898 - On April 25, the United States entered the Spanish-American War with Spain; the two nations signed the Treaty of Paris on December 10.

1900 - McKinley was reelected president of the United States.

1901 - On September 6, assassin Leon F. Czolgosz shot McKinley at the Pan-American Exposition in Buffalo, New York; on September 14, William McKinley died.

DID YOU KNOW?

Several U.S. presidents served in the American Civil War. William McKinley was the last of these men to become president.

McKinley signed the Gold Standard Act into law with a special gold pen.

Today, McKinley and his wife are buried at the McKinley National Memorial in Canton, Ohio.

McKinley always wore a red carnation in the buttonhole of his coat.

GROWING UP IN OHIO

William McKinley was born in Niles, Ohio, on January 29, 1843. He was the seventh of nine children born to William and Nancy Allison McKinley. William's father managed an iron **foundry**. His mother was a strong, energetic community leader. Young William was good at playing marbles. He was also an excellent shot with his bow and arrows. Most of all, William liked to make and fly kites.

William's parents wanted their children to have a good education. So in 1852, the family moved. They settled in Poland, Ohio, where there were better schools. At Poland Academy, William showed a great gift for public speaking. He became president of the Everett Literary and **Debating** Society.

FAST FACTS

BORN - January 29, 1843
WIFE - Ida Saxton
     (1847–1907)
CHILDREN - 2
POLITICAL PARTY - Republican
AGE AT INAUGURATION - 54
YEARS SERVED - 1897–1901
VICE PRESIDENTS - Garret A. Hobart,
          Theodore Roosevelt
DIED - September 14, 1901, age 58

William and Nancy Allison McKinley

At age 17, William attended Allegheny College in Meadville, Pennsylvania. But soon, he got sick and had to return home. William then taught at Kerr School near Poland. He also worked as a clerk at the post office.

CIVIL WAR HERO

During the 1850s, problems were growing between the Northern and Southern states. The South wanted slavery and the North did not. The Southern states eventually separated from the Northern states. They formed the Confederate States of America.

These events led to the American **Civil War**, which began in April 1861. In June, McKinley joined the Twenty-third Ohio Volunteer **Infantry** as a private. He served under future president Rutherford B. Hayes. Later, Hayes encouraged McKinley's political career.

On September 17, 1862, McKinley participated in the Battle of Antietam. McKinley was in charge of the food supplies for his fellow soldiers. He braved enemy fire to bring them food during the battle.

McKinley survived one of the deadliest single-day battles of the Civil War. More than 20,000 soldiers died in the Battle of Antietam.

Rutherford B. Hayes was president from 1877 to 1881.

Because of his bravery, McKinley was promoted to the rank of second lieutenant. His courage and hard work continued. When the war ended, McKinley held the rank of **brevet** major.

After the war, McKinley returned to Poland. There, he studied law at the office of Judge Charles E. Glidden. He also studied at the Albany Law School in Albany, New York.

In 1867, McKinley became a lawyer and began practicing law in Canton, Ohio. He opened a small office in the town's new bank building. McKinley did well as a lawyer. He soon became a partner in George W. Belden's law practice.

POLITICS AND FAMILY

In 1869, McKinley was elected **prosecuting attorney** of Stark County, Ohio. He often defended and spoke out for unpopular causes. McKinley helped African Americans by defending their right to vote.

McKinley was also the only lawyer who would defend a group of miners. They had gone on strike and were accused of destroying company property. McKinley took the case for free. He proved most of the men innocent.

While in Canton, McKinley met Ida Saxton. She was the daughter of a wealthy banker. Ida worked as a cashier in her father's bank.

McKinley and Ida married on January 25, 1871. On December 25, the couple had a daughter they named Katherine. Their daughter Ida was born on April 1, 1873.

After Ida's birth, several sad events occurred. In 1873, Mrs. McKinley's mother died. The same year, baby Ida died when she was just a few months old. Then in June 1875, three-year-old Katherine died.

The McKinleys were filled with sorrow. McKinley continued his career in politics. But his wife was unhappy. She became sickly and suffered from **seizures** for the rest of her life. Throughout his career, McKinley remained devoted to and protective of his wife.

Ida McKinley was seen as an excellent judge of people and political events.

CONGRESSMAN MCKINLEY

In 1876, McKinley was elected to the U.S. House of Representatives. He began serving the following year. McKinley was a hardworking, honest congressman. He voted for the Chinese Exclusion Act of 1882. This limited Chinese **immigration** for ten years.

In 1883, McKinley voted for the Pendleton **Civil Service** Act. Before this, people were given civil service jobs based on their political party. The new act required people to pass tests to get these jobs instead.

McKinley also supported the Dependent Pension Act, which passed in 1890. The act provided money to **veterans** of the American **Civil War** if they ever became disabled.

Ohio senator George H. Pendleton sponsored the Pendleton Civil Service Act.

[Public No 71]

Congress of the United States, At the First Session,

Begun and held at the CITY OF WASHINGTON, in the DISTRICT OF COLUMBIA, on Monday, the fifth day of December, eighteen hundred and eighty one

An Act

To execute certain treaty stipulations relating to Chinese.

Whereas, In the opinion of the Government of the United States the coming of Chinese laborers to this country endangers the good order of certain localities within the territory thereof: Therefore, Be it enacted by the Senate and House of Representatives of the United States of America in Congress assembled, That from and after the expiration of ninety days next after the passage of this act, and until the expiration of ten years next after the passage of this act, the coming of Chinese laborers to the United States be, and the same is hereby, suspended; and during such suspension it shall not be lawful for any Chinese laborer to come, or, having so come after the expiration of said ninety days, to remain within the United States.

Sec. 2. That the master of any vessel who shall knowingly bring within the United States on such vessel, and land or permit to be landed, any Chinese laborer, from any foreign port or place, shall be deemed guilty of a misdemeanor, and on conviction thereof shall be punished by a fine of not more than five hundred dollars for each and every such Chinese laborer so brought, and may be also imprisoned for a term not exceeding one year.

Sec. 3. That the two foregoing sections shall not apply to Chinese laborers who were in the United States on the seventeenth day of November, eighteen hundred and eighty, or who shall have come into the same before the expiration of ninety days next after the passage of this act, and who shall produce

... any vessel of any Chinese person not lawfully entitled to ... the United States, shall be deemed guilty of a misdemeanor, ... shall, on conviction thereof, be fined in a sum not exceeding ... thousand dollars, and imprisoned for a term not exceeding one ...

... That no Chinese person shall be permitted to enter the United ... by land without producing to the proper officer of customs the ... certificate in this act required of Chinese persons seeking to land from ... And any Chinese person found unlawfully within the United ... shall be caused to be removed therefrom to the country from when ... by direction of the President of the United States, and at the ... the United States, after being brought before some justice, judge, ... commissioner of a court of the United States and found to be one ... lawfully entitled to be or remain in the United States.

... That this act shall not apply to diplomatic and other officers ... Chinese Government traveling upon the business of that gov... whose credentials shall be taken as equivalent to the certi... this act mentioned, and shall exempt them and their body and ... servants from the provisions of this act as to other Chinese persons.

... That hereafter no State court or court of the United States ... Chinese to citizenship; and all laws in conflict with this act are ...

... the words "Chinese laborers," wherever used in this act, shall be ... mean both skilled and unskilled laborers and Chinese employed ...

J. Warren Keifer
Speaker of the House of Representatives.

David Davis
President of the Senate, pro tempore.

Approved May 6, 1882.

Chester A. Arthur

President Chester Arthur signed the Chinese Exclusion Act.

In Congress, McKinley served on the Committee on Revision of the Laws. He also became chairman of the House Ways and Means Committee. This group focuses on how to raise the money necessary to run the government.

As chairman, McKinley sponsored the McKinley **Tariff** Act of 1890. This law put high taxes on foreign products sold in the United States.

McKinley thought the act would improve the nation's **economy**. Businesses liked this new law. However, many Americans did not like paying more for products. Partly because the act was so unpopular, McKinley was not reelected in 1890.

Despite losing the election, McKinley remained a strong candidate for public office. So, the **Republicans** nominated him for governor of Ohio. McKinley easily won the election in 1891. He was reelected in 1893.

During this time, Governor McKinley improved the state's canals and roads. He also passed laws to tax railroads as well as telegraph and telephone operators. Foreign companies that did business in Ohio faced new tax laws, too.

While McKinley was governor, he continued to support the Republican Party. He made hundreds of speeches for Republican candidates for Congress in 1894.

THE ELECTION OF 1896

McKinley was popular in the **Republican** Party. At the 1896 **Republican National Convention** in Saint Louis, Missouri, he was nominated to run for president. Garret A. Hobart of New Jersey became McKinley's **running mate**.

McKinley's opponent was **Democrat** William Jennings Bryan of Nebraska. Bryan's running mate was Arthur Sewall of Maine.

Garret A. Hobart had served in the New Jersey state legislature.

McKinley and Bryan ran their campaigns very differently. Bryan traveled across the country to make speeches and meet his supporters.

Meanwhile, McKinley stayed home. From there, he greeted the thousands of supporters who came to Canton. This became known as the "front porch campaign."

McKinley made campaign speeches from his home in Canton, Ohio.

In 1913, William Jennings Bryan became secretary of state in President Woodrow Wilson's cabinet.

The biggest issue of the election was America's money system. McKinley supported the gold standard. This meant that paper money could be traded in for a specific amount of gold. Bryan backed the free silver system. This would allow an unlimited number of silver coins to be made. However, silver was not worth as much as gold.

The free silver system would increase the money supply. So, Bryan had the support of the poor and those in **debt**. Farmers also liked the plan. They hoped to charge more for their crops. However, McKinley said this was not good for consumers. He had the backing of bankers and businessmen.

In November 1896, McKinley easily won the election. He defeated Bryan by almost 600,000 **popular votes**. McKinley received 271 electoral votes to Bryan's 176 votes.

The same year, the **Republican** Party gained control of the Senate and the House. The party would remain in power for the next 14 years.

McKinley and Hobart supported the gold standard and a high tariff.

PRESIDENT MCKINLEY

President McKinley took office in 1897. At the time, the island of Cuba was controlled by Spain. Yet the Cubans wanted freedom from Spanish rule. There was a chance that war could break out.

At this time, there were many Americans living in Cuba. Concerned for their safety, the United States sent the battleship USS *Maine* to Cuba. On February 15, 1898, the *Maine* exploded and sank. The incident killed 266 military men.

Most people believed Spain had blown up the ship. But President McKinley was against war with Spain. So, he ordered an investigation. The report stated that the explosion was not an accident. Yet today, some people think it was.

On April 25, 1898, the United States declared war on Spain. The United States quickly won the Spanish-American War. The two countries then signed the Treaty of Paris on December 10.

PRESIDENT McKINLEY'S CABINET

FIRST TERM
MARCH 4, 1897– MARCH 4, 1901

STATE – John Sherman
  William R. Day (from April 28, 1898)
  John Hay (from September 30, 1898)
TREASURY – Lyman J. Gage
WAR – Russell A. Alger
  Elihu Root (from August 1, 1899)
NAVY – John D. Long
ATTORNEY GENERAL – Joseph McKenna
  John W. Griggs (from February 1, 1898)
INTERIOR – Cornelius N. Bliss
  Ethan A. Hitchcock (from February 20, 1899)
AGRICULTURE – James Wilson

SECOND TERM
MARCH 4, 1901– SEPTEMBER 14, 1901

STATE – John Hay
TREASURY – Lyman J. Gage
WAR – Elihu Root
NAVY – John D. Long
ATTORNEY GENERAL – John W. Griggs
  Philander C. Knox (from April 10, 1901)
INTERIOR – Ethan A. Hitchcock
AGRICULTURE – James Wilson

Throughout his presidency, McKinley focused on foreign relations.

The Treaty of Paris freed Cuba from Spanish control. It also gave the United States more territory. The nation acquired Puerto Rico, Guam, and the Philippines.

While McKinley was in office, the United States also claimed other territories. It **annexed** the Hawaiian Islands in 1898. In 1899, it split the Samoa Islands with Germany. The same year, the United States acquired Wake Island in the Pacific Ocean.

The United States had gained a lot of territory. Now, the U.S. Navy would benefit from easy access to both the Atlantic and Pacific oceans. So, President McKinley supported what became the Hay-Pauncefote Treaty. The treaty gave the United States ownership of the future **Panama Canal**. It passed after McKinley's death.

Throughout his presidency, McKinley supported a variety of important legislation. He signed the Dingley **Tariff** Act on July 24, 1897. It allowed him to **negotiate** taxes for certain foreign goods.

On March 14, 1900, President McKinley signed the Gold Standard Act. It established gold as the standard of currency. The same year, McKinley sent troops to China. They went to help end the **Boxer Rebellion**.

SUPREME
COURT
APPOINTMENT

JOSEPH McKENNA - 1898

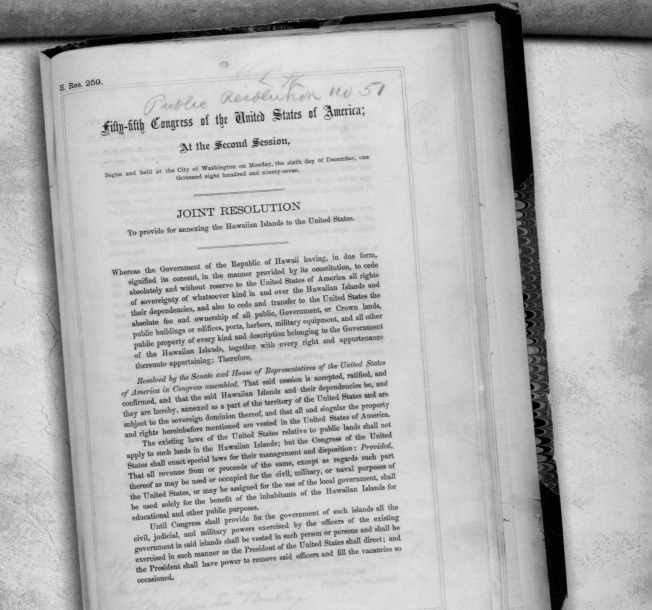

Public Resolution no 51

Fifty-fifth Congress of the United States of America;

At the Second Session,

Begun and held at the City of Washington on Monday, the sixth day of December, one thousand eight hundred and ninety-seven.

JOINT RESOLUTION

To provide for annexing the Hawaiian Islands to the United States.

Whereas the Government of the Republic of Hawaii having, in due form, signified its consent, in the manner provided by its constitution, to cede absolutely and without reserve to the United States of America all rights of sovereignty of whatsoever kind in and over the Hawaiian Islands and their dependencies, and also to cede and transfer to the United States the absolute fee and ownership of all public, Government, or Crown lands, public buildings or edifices, ports, harbors, military equipment, and all other public property of every kind and description belonging to the Government of the Hawaiian Islands, together with every right and appurtenance thereunto appertaining: Therefore,

Resolved by the Senate and House of Representatives of the United States of America in Congress assembled, That said cession is accepted, ratified, and confirmed, and that the said Hawaiian Islands and their dependencies be, and they are hereby, annexed as a part of the territory of the United States and are subject to the sovereign dominion thereof, and that all and singular the property and rights hereinbefore mentioned are vested in the United States of America.

The existing laws of the United States relative to public lands shall not apply to such lands in the Hawaiian Islands; but the Congress of the United States shall enact special laws for their management and disposition : *Provided,* That all revenue from or proceeds of the same, except as regards such part thereof as may be used or occupied for the civil, military, or naval purposes of the United States, or may be assigned for the use of the local government, shall be used solely for the benefit of the inhabitants of the Hawaiian Islands for educational and other public purposes.

Until Congress shall provide for the government of such islands all the civil, judicial, and military powers exercised by the officers of the existing government in said islands shall be vested in such person or persons and shall be exercised in such manner as the President of the United States shall direct; and the President shall have power to remove said officers and fill the vacancies so occasioned.

Congress annexed the Hawaiian Islands in July 1898.

A TRAGIC ENDING

McKinley and Roosevelt earned nearly 900,000 more popular votes than their opponents.

In 1900, President McKinley ran for reelection. Vice President Hobart had died in office the year before. He had not been replaced. The **Republicans** chose New York governor Theodore Roosevelt as McKinley's new **running mate**.

Once again, McKinley ran against William Jennings Bryan. Bryan's **running mate** was former vice president Adlai E. Stevenson. McKinley and Roosevelt easily won the election. This time, McKinley received 292 electoral votes to Bryan's 155 votes.

President McKinley then began a trip through the western states. He concluded the tour in New York. There, the Pan-American Exposition was taking place in Buffalo.

On September 5, 1901, President McKinley spoke at the Pan-American Exposition. More than 50,000 people listened to his speech!

On September 6, 1901, President McKinley was attending the Pan-American Exposition. At a reception at the Temple of Music, hundreds of people waited to shake his hand. Anarchist Leon F. Czolgosz was among the guests.

Hidden under a handkerchief, Czolgosz held a gun. When President McKinley reached to shake his hand, Czolgosz fired the gun twice. One bullet bounced off a button but entered McKinley's chest. The other bullet wounded him in the stomach.

Construction began on the McKinley National Memorial on June 6, 1905. It was completed by September 1907, just six years after McKinley's death.

OHIO
HISTORICAL
MARKER

THE MCKINLEY NATIONAL MEMORIAL

William McKinley served the nation as president, the people of Ohio as governor, and the citizens of his congressional district as a representative. McKinley was shot by an assassin in Buffalo, New York, in September 1901 and died several days later. The McKinley National Memorial, funded by children's donations, was dedicated in 1907. It is the burial site of the 25th President, First Lady Ida Saxton McKinley, and two daughters. Designed by architect Harold ... Milford granite structure ...

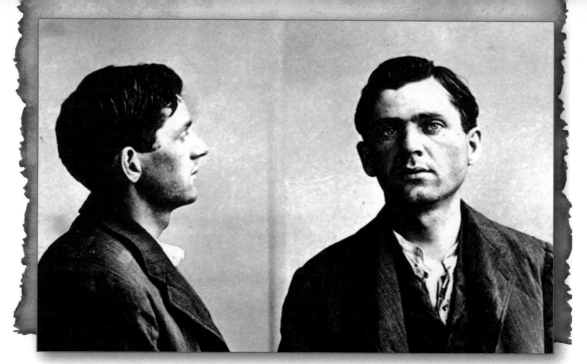

Leon F. Czolgosz went to trial and was found guilty of McKinley's murder. He was executed on October 29, 1901.

At first, everyone was hopeful the president would recover. Sadly, William McKinley died eight days later on September 14, 1901. His last words were, "Good-bye, all. It is God's way. His will, not ours be done."

McKinley was buried in Canton, Ohio. His devotion to his wife and his kind nature earned him respect. William McKinley holds an important place in U.S. history for the territories acquired during his presidency.

OFFICE OF THE PRESIDENT

BRANCHES OF GOVERNMENT

The U.S. government is divided into three branches. They are the executive, legislative, and judicial branches. This division is called a separation of powers. Each branch has some power over the others. This is called a system of checks and balances.

EXECUTIVE BRANCH

The executive branch enforces laws. It is made up of the president, the vice president, and the president's cabinet. The president represents the United States around the world. He or she oversees relations with other countries and signs treaties. The president signs bills into law and appoints officials and federal judges. He or she also leads the military and manages government workers.

LEGISLATIVE BRANCH

The legislative branch makes laws, maintains the military, and regulates trade. It also has the power to declare war. This branch consists of the Senate and the House of Representatives. Together, these two houses make up Congress. Each state has two senators. A state's population determines the number of representatives it has.

JUDICIAL BRANCH

The judicial branch interprets laws. It consists of district courts, courts of appeals, and the Supreme Court. District courts try cases. If a person disagrees with a trial's outcome, he or she may appeal. If the courts of appeals support the ruling, a person may appeal to the Supreme Court. The Supreme Court also makes sure that laws follow the U.S. Constitution.

QUALIFICATIONS FOR OFFICE

To be president, a person must meet three requirements. A candidate must be at least 35 years old and a natural-born U.S. citizen. He or she must also have lived in the United States for at least 14 years.

ELECTORAL COLLEGE

The U.S. presidential election is an indirect election. Voters from each state choose electors to represent them in the Electoral College. The number of electors from each state is based on population. Each elector has one electoral vote. Electors are pledged to cast their vote for the candidate who receives the highest number of popular votes in their state. A candidate must receive the majority of Electoral College votes to win.

TERM OF OFFICE

Each president may be elected to two four-year terms. Sometimes, a president may only be elected once. This happens if he or she served more than two years of the previous president's term.

The presidential election is held on the Tuesday after the first Monday in November. The president is sworn in on January 20 of the following year. At that time, he or she takes the oath of office:

I do solemnly swear (or affirm) that I will faithfully execute the office of President of the United States, and will to the best of my ability, preserve, protect and defend the Constitution of the United States.

LINE OF SUCCESSION

The Presidential Succession Act of 1947 defines who becomes president if the president cannot serve. The vice president is first in the line of succession. Next are the Speaker of the House and the President Pro Tempore of the Senate. If none of these individuals is able to serve, the office falls to the president's cabinet members. They would take office in the order in which each department was created:

Secretary of State

Secretary of the Treasury

Secretary of Defense

Attorney General

Secretary of the Interior

Secretary of Agriculture

Secretary of Commerce

Secretary of Labor

Secretary of Health and Human Services

Secretary of Housing and Urban Development

Secretary of Transportation

Secretary of Energy

Secretary of Education

Secretary of Veterans Affairs

Secretary of Homeland Security

BENEFITS

• While in office, the president receives a salary of $400,000 each year. He or she lives in the White House and has 24-hour Secret Service protection.

• The president may travel on a Boeing 747 jet called Air Force One. The airplane can accommodate 70 passengers. It has kitchens, a dining room, sleeping areas, and a conference room. It also has fully equipped offices with the latest communications systems. Air Force One can fly halfway around the world before needing to refuel. It can even refuel in flight!

• If the president wishes to travel by car, he or she uses Cadillac One. Cadillac One is a Cadillac Deville. It has been modified with heavy armor and communications systems. The president takes Cadillac One along when visiting other countries if secure transportation will be needed.

• The president also travels on a helicopter called Marine One. Like the presidential car, Marine One accompanies the president when traveling abroad if necessary.

• Sometimes, the president needs to get away and relax with family and friends. Camp David is the official presidential retreat. It is located in the cool, wooded mountains in Maryland. The U.S. Navy maintains the retreat, and the U.S. Marine Corps keeps it secure. The camp offers swimming, tennis, golf, and hiking.

• When the president leaves office, he or she receives Secret Service protection for ten more years. He or she also receives a yearly pension of $191,300 and funding for office space, supplies, and staff.

PRESIDENTS AND THEIR TERMS

PRESIDENT	PARTY	TOOK OFFICE	LEFT OFFICE	TERMS SERVED	VICE PRESIDENT
George Washington	None	April 30, 1789	March 4, 1797	Two	John Adams
John Adams	Federalist	March 4, 1797	March 4, 1801	One	Thomas Jefferson
Thomas Jefferson	Democratic-Republican	March 4, 1801	March 4, 1809	Two	Aaron Burr, George Clinton
James Madison	Democratic-Republican	March 4, 1809	March 4, 1817	Two	George Clinton, Elbridge Gerry
James Monroe	Democratic-Republican	March 4, 1817	March 4, 1825	Two	Daniel D. Tompkins
John Quincy Adams	Democratic-Republican	March 4, 1825	March 4, 1829	One	John C. Calhoun
Andrew Jackson	Democrat	March 4, 1829	March 4, 1837	Two	John C. Calhoun, Martin Van Buren
Martin Van Buren	Democrat	March 4, 1837	March 4, 1841	One	Richard M. Johnson
William H. Harrison	Whig	March 4, 1841	April 4, 1841	Died During First Term	John Tyler
John Tyler	Whig	April 6, 1841	March 4, 1845	Completed Harrison's Term	Office Vacant
James K. Polk	Democrat	March 4, 1845	March 4, 1849	One	George M. Dallas
Zachary Taylor	Whig	March 5, 1849	July 9, 1850	Died During First Term	Millard Fillmore

PRESIDENT	PARTY	TOOK OFFICE	LEFT OFFICE	TERMS SERVED	VICE PRESIDENT
Millard Fillmore	Whig	July 10, 1850	March 4, 1853	Completed Taylor's Term	Office Vacant
Franklin Pierce	Democrat	March 4, 1853	March 4, 1857	One	William R.D. King
James Buchanan	Democrat	March 4, 1857	March 4, 1861	One	John C. Breckinridge
Abraham Lincoln	Republican	March 4, 1861	April 15, 1865	Served One Term, Died During Second Term	Hannibal Hamlin, Andrew Johnson
Andrew Johnson	Democrat	April 15, 1865	March 4, 1869	Completed Lincoln's Second Term	Office Vacant
Ulysses S. Grant	Republican	March 4, 1869	March 4, 1877	Two	Schuyler Colfax, Henry Wilson
Rutherford B. Hayes	Republican	March 3, 1877	March 4, 1881	One	William A. Wheeler
James A. Garfield	Republican	March 4, 1881	September 19, 1881	Died During First Term	Chester Arthur
Chester Arthur	Republican	September 20, 1881	March 4, 1885	Completed Garfield's Term	Office Vacant
Grover Cleveland	Democrat	March 4, 1885	March 4, 1889	One	Thomas A. Hendricks
Benjamin Harrison	Republican	March 4, 1889	March 4, 1893	One	Levi P. Morton
Grover Cleveland	Democrat	March 4, 1893	March 4, 1897	One	Adlai E. Stevenson
William McKinley	Republican	March 4, 1897	September 14, 1901	Served One Term, Died During Second Term	Garret A. Hobart, Theodore Roosevelt

PRESIDENT	PARTY	TOOK OFFICE	LEFT OFFICE	TERMS SERVED	VICE PRESIDENT
Theodore Roosevelt	Republican	September 14, 1901	March 4, 1909	Completed McKinley's Second Term, Served One Term	Office Vacant, Charles Fairbanks
William Taft	Republican	March 4, 1909	March 4, 1913	One	James S. Sherman
Woodrow Wilson	Democrat	March 4, 1913	March 4, 1921	Two	Thomas R. Marshall
Warren G. Harding	Republican	March 4, 1921	August 2, 1923	Died During First Term	Calvin Coolidge
Calvin Coolidge	Republican	August 3, 1923	March 4, 1929	Completed Harding's Term, Served One Term	Office Vacant, Charles Dawes
Herbert Hoover	Republican	March 4, 1929	March 4, 1933	One	Charles Curtis
Franklin D. Roosevelt	Democrat	March 4, 1933	April 12, 1945	Served Three Terms, Died During Fourth Term	John Nance Garner, Henry A. Wallace, Harry S. Truman
Harry S. Truman	Democrat	April 12, 1945	January 20, 1953	Completed Roosevelt's Fourth Term, Served One Term	Office Vacant, Alben Barkley
Dwight D. Eisenhower	Republican	January 20, 1953	January 20, 1961	Two	Richard Nixon
John F. Kennedy	Democrat	January 20, 1961	November 22, 1963	Died During First Term	Lyndon B. Johnson
Lyndon B. Johnson	Democrat	November 22, 1963	January 20, 1969	Completed Kennedy's Term, Served One Term	Office Vacant, Hubert H. Humphrey
Richard Nixon	Republican	January 20, 1969	August 9, 1974	Completed First Term, Resigned During Second Term	Spiro T. Agnew, Gerald Ford

PRESIDENTS 26–37, 1901–1974

PRESIDENT	PARTY	TOOK OFFICE	LEFT OFFICE	TERMS SERVED	VICE PRESIDENT
Gerald Ford	Republican	August 9, 1974	January 20, 1977	Completed Nixon's Second Term	Nelson A. Rockefeller
Jimmy Carter	Democrat	January 20, 1977	January 20, 1981	One	Walter Mondale
Ronald Reagan	Republican	January 20, 1981	January 20, 1989	Two	George H.W. Bush
George H.W. Bush	Republican	January 20, 1989	January 20, 1993	One	Dan Quayle
Bill Clinton	Democrat	January 20, 1993	January 20, 2001	Two	Al Gore
George W. Bush	Republican	January 20, 2001	January 20, 2009	Two	Dick Cheney
Barack Obama	Democrat	January 20, 2009			Joe Biden

"Equality of rights must prevail, and our laws be always and everywhere respected and obeyed." William McKinley

WRITE TO THE PRESIDENT

You may write to the president at:

**The White House
1600 Pennsylvania Avenue NW
Washington, DC 20500**

You may e-mail the president at:

comments@whitehouse.gov

GLOSSARY

annex - to take land and add it to a nation.

assassinate - to murder a very important person, usually for political reasons.

Boxer Rebellion - in 1900, an uprising in which Chinese peasants tried to force all foreigners from China.

brevet - a military title given to an officer who has a higher rank than he or she is paid for.

civil service - the part of the government that is responsible for matters not covered by the military, the courts, or the law.

civil war - a war between groups in the same country. The United States of America and the Confederate States of America fought a civil war from 1861 to 1865.

debate - a contest in which two sides argue for or against something.

debt - something owed to someone, usually money.

Democrat - a member of the Democratic political party. When William McKinley was president, Democrats supported farmers and landowners.

economy - the way a nation uses its money, goods, and natural resources.

foundry - a place where metals are cast.

immigration - entry into another country to live. A person who immigrates is called an immigrant.

infantry - soldiers trained and organized to fight on foot.

negotiate (nih-GOH-shee-ayt) - to work out an agreement about the terms of a contract.

Panama Canal - a human-made, narrow canal across Panama that connects the Atlantic and Pacific oceans.

popular vote - the vote of the entire body of people with the right to vote.

prosecuting attorney - a lawyer who represents the government in criminal cases.

Republican - a member of the Republican political party. When William McKinley was president, Republicans supported business and strong government.

Republican National Convention - a national meeting held every four years during which the Republican Party chooses its candidates for president and vice president.

running mate - a candidate running for a lower-rank position on an election ticket, especially the candidate for vice president.

seizure (SEE-zhuhr) - an episode of disturbed brain function that causes changes in attention and behavior.

tariff - the taxes a government puts on imported or exported goods.

veteran - a person who has served in the armed forces.

WEB SITES

To learn more about William McKinley, visit ABDO Publishing Company on the World Wide Web at **www.abdopublishing.com**. Web sites about William McKinley are featured on our Book Links page. These links are routinely monitored and updated to provide the most current information available.

INDEX